C000283873

BRITAIN IN OLD PHOTOGRAPHS

LOWESTOFT
PAST & PRESENT

IAN G. ROBB

SUTTON PUBLISHING LIMITED

Sutton Publishing Limited
Phoenix Mill · Thrupp · Stroud
Gloucestershire · GL5 2BU

First published 2000

Reprinted in 2002, 2005

Copyright © Ian G. Robb, 2000

Title page photograph: London Road North,
c. 1910, *see* page 41.

British Library Cataloguing in Publication Data
A catalogue record for this book is available from the
British Library.

ISBN 0-7509-2380-6

Typeset in 10.5/13.5 Photina.
Typesetting and origination by
Sutton Publishing Limited.
Printed and bound in England by
J.H. Haynes & Co. Ltd, Sparkford.

The Esplanade, 1938. There is a
marked difference in styles
between the three young ladies
dressed in the height of summer
fashion walking past Wellington
Gardens and the pair they have
just passed. The weather cannot
have been inclement as two of
the girls are barefoot!

CONTENTS

London Road North from the Marina, looking towards Gordon Road, *c.* 1948. Weeds had covered much of the site damaged in the Waller raid of 1942. The steeple between the chimneys belonged to the Central Methodist church. Only one car is in sight. Post-war austerity meant that cycling was the order of the day. (*Waveney District Council*)

INTRODUCTION

O ver the centuries Lowestoft has seen many changes and history has left its mark, notably in the last 150 years. Described in the town's official guide for 1910 as the 'Queen of East Coast Watering Places', two world wars, the clearances of the 1960s, the decline of the fishing industry and the various road systems – notably on the north side of the Bridge – have altered the town in one way or another. Lowestoft expanded slowly at first, gathering momentum in the years before 1914, and in the last two decades of the twentieth century has seen private and housing association estates stretching the boundaries of the town into what had once been outlying villages.

For centuries Lowestoft was a small town approximately a mile in length facing the German Ocean, today's North Sea, on top of a gently sloping cliff. Fish-houses and stores were at the foot of these cliffs and the vessels themselves were pulled up on to the beach. The town thrived on the herring and mackerel fisheries, and from its seafaring tradition there came several naval heroes, notably in the Dutch and French wars of the seventeenth and eighteenth centuries; the most famous, Sir Thomas Allin, Elder Brother of Trinity House, was a contemporary and friend of Samuel Pepys. By the latter half of the eighteenth century the town had become a fashionable resort with the gentry and nobility who had discovered the restorative effects of its waters, the beach and its bracing air. Paving and the London toll-road were part of the ensuing improvements which continued into the 1830s with the town's first bridge – built as part of an enterprise to link Norwich with the sea via Lowestoft.

Sir Samuel Morton Peto made the greatest impact on the town prior to the twentieth century. Responsible for developing the harbour and bringing the railway to Lowestoft, he also built the New Town Estate on wasteland between the Bridge and Kirkley, and with the aid of his architects John Thomas and John Louth Clemence turned Lowestoft into a superior resort and important commercial and fishing port.

Much of present-day Lowestoft is the result of post-war reconstruction, redevelopment and attempts to come to terms with the motor car. As the most easterly point in Britain, and therefore the nearest town to Germany, Lowestoft suffered considerably during the Second World War. Shipyards, munition factories and the port were all targeted by enemy aircraft.

The clearing of slum areas had started before the last war. New municipal housing such as the Roman Hill Estate began in the late 1920s. The Beach village, part of the fishing life of the town since the early nineteenth century, was declared a slum area in the mid-1930s, and a start was made later in the decade replacing the old cottages at the foot of Lighthouse Score. With hindsight, however, it was fortunate that the war intervened at that point. There had been plans to replace the old Beach with a housing estate, but it is doubtful that this estate would have survived beyond the Floods of 1953, which sounded the death-knell of the village as it was.

The rehousing of Lowestoft's bombed-out population led firstly to the building of the Gunton Estate, laid out in 1945, then later the Whitton Estate, and finally the Beeches Estate in the mid-1950s. But the most dramatic change in the post-war years was the clearance in the 1960s of the older parts of Lowestoft. Regretfully, it also saw the destruction of an important chapter in the town's history. Some 400 years were wiped off the map with the loss of ancient houses and thoroughfares including Duke's Head Street, Dove Street, White Horse Street and much of Mariner's Street, the latter containing what is now considered to be the town's oldest building.

The construction of the North Lowestoft spinal relief road brought the most changes in the last thirty years. Katwijk Way and Jubilee Way split the town north of the Bridge into two. South of the Bridge, however, it has been the changes in holidaymakers' habits and the loss, among other things, of the South Pier Pavilion. The closure of factories such as Morton's, the Cooperative Canning factory, Pye and Richards' shipyard – all on the south side of the Bridge – caused major employment problems which are still with us. In recent years, however, Kirkley has started to benefit through its long-term regeneration scheme, and the resort has also regained some of its former glory. The only thing that has not changed is that Lowestoft still has only one bridge linking the two halves of the town.

Over the last twenty-five years Lowestoft's fishing fleet has shrunk to a microcosm of what it once was. At one time it was the town's major industry, but today only a small number of vessels fish from the port. The market's 4,000 ft of quay was usually fairly full in the 1960s; today much of what survives is given over to other uses.

In our journey through Lowestoft Past and Present, with only the odd exception I have placed yesterday and today either on the same page or on facing pages, comparing like with like. I find it difficult to believe that I have been behind a camera for the best part of two and a half decades: most of the photographs between 1975 and 1990 were taken by me. Today's scenes were taken by me specially for this book and are as near as possible to the location of yesteryear – traffic permitting.

I hope that this book will bring back memories – some recent, some long forgotten.

CHAPTER ONE

THE HIGH STREET AREA

O'Doherty's dental surgery and the Nest Garage, themselves the result of street widening in the late 1890s and seen here in the early autumn of 1976, were among premises in the upper part of the High Street that were soon to be demolished to make way for Jubilee Way, part of the town's spinal relief road.

Sparrow's Nest, *c.* 1910. Apart from the 'Refreshments' banner, the house is seen possibly much as Robert Sparrow of Worlingham Hall, who used it as his summer home, may have known it. The house and lands had been bought by the Corporation in 1897 and turned into pleasure gardens. The Navy took over the Nest during the Second World War, and the old house disappeared forever, hidden by war-time buildings.

Sparrow's Nest Theatre, winter 1989. Built as a pavilion in 1913 to replace a marquee, throughout the years a galaxy of stars including classical pianist Mark Hambourg, singer Donald Peers – who started his career at the Nest – and comedian Frankie Howerd appeared here. By the late 1980s the building was badly in need of repair and, despite attempts to save it, was demolished in 1991.

Dress rehearsal, Sparrow's Nest Theatre, early 1978. The theatre was also a favourite with amateurs, for instance the annual Gang Show, when scouts, guides, cubs and brownies were brought together by the late Jack Overy to display their various talents on the stage. These three girls, however, seem to anticipate their turn with some trepidation.

Today all has changed – although the wartime buildings, parts of which house the Lowestoft War Memorial Museum and the RNPS Museum, remain. The Nest's theatre has been replaced by a wide lawn between the Ciné Club and the Sparrow's Nest bar. The house itself was pulled down in the early 1960s. Only part of the outer walls now remain.

Lowestoft High Light, *c.* 1867. Built in 1676 by order of Samuel Pepys on the advice of Sir Thomas Allin, it was located at the highest point north of the High Street. In the 1770s the light was changed from coal to oil, and over the years the lighthouse was enlarged to the size seen here. The walls to the left behind the gas lamp belong to the Sparrow's Nest, known then as Cliff Cottage.

Lowestoft High Light today. Built in 1873 on the foundations of the earlier lighthouse, the tower was heightened to some 123 ft above sea level. Its paraffin oil light was first turned on in 1874; electrification eventually arrived in 1936. Automated in 1975, part of the station is now a private house.

No. 1 High Street, not long after the Second World War. A large crack seen over the upper window nearest the camera was the result of damage caused by shelling. The house was thought to have been built towards the end of the eighteenth century and was the home in the mid-nineteenth century of Captain Preston RN. Between the wars a local JP, Miss B.M. Doughty, lived there.

The site today, looking across to the North Sea from the junction of St Margaret's Road. The house was demolished in the late 1950s and its site is now part of Arnold Walk. A bus stop marks where the house once stood; the shelter stands approximately on what had been the path leading to the house.

Nest Garage and Belle Vue public house, junction of St Margaret's Road and High Street, October 1976. Built as the result of road widening in about 1900, the garage retained vestiges of its early Edwardian self up to the 1970s, including a cycling club plaque on the front of the building. Petrol was delivered from pumps hung over the pavement. The Belle Vue next door was built in 1903 to replace the Three Herrings.

The Nest Garage, Belle Vue public house and other premises were cleared in 1976 to make way for the new spinal road which meets the High Street just north of what had been the junction of St Margaret's Road. Parkholme Terrace cottages, whose back-yards face the camera, are all that now remain of this side of the High Street. Stradbroke House is on the left.

Jubilee Way, summer 1977. The North Lowestoft spinal relief road seen from the junction of St Margaret's Road and looking towards Camden Street and Albany Road. Stradbroke House (left) is in the High Street, Osborne Street is the terrace on the right. The much-needed route separated the High Street from the rest of the town.

Jubilee Way, the upper end of the North Lowestoft spinal relief route, seen today from what had been the junction of St Margaret's Road. The petrol sign (centre left) indicates the High Street filling station. There is no terrace in Camden Street; the roofs are those in Albany Road. The Osborne Street terrace appears to have changed little in this rare moment of calm on an otherwise busy road.

Ancient houses on the corner of the Hemplands and Osborne Street, 1976. In the background can be seen part of the Tricentrol garage in the High Street. The Hemplands, once an important part of Lowestoft, supplied the raw material to make rope for the town's ships and fishing industry. Osborne Street, on the other hand, was comparatively recent, having only been laid out in the early 1900s.

Nowadays Jubilee Way ploughs through what had once been the east side of the Hemplands, separating this part of north Lowestoft from the High Street. Beyond the brick wall concealing the traffic is the eastern part of Osborne Street, now Belle Vue Close. The High Street itself lies between the filling station (centre) and the trees of the High Street gardens. Pearson's the builders is the corner block on the right.

Tricentrol Garage, High Street, September 1986. Originally built in the mid-1920s for P.W. Watson on the site of the Cunningham School, it was used by the Royal Navy during the war until destroyed by bombing. It was rebuilt in the 1950s and remodelled in the 1970s. To the left is Camden Street, which from 1978 became part of the one-way system linking south-bound traffic in the High Street to Jubilee Way.

A filling station replaced the old garage in the late 1980s, and is now part of an island surrounded by a sea of traffic. The houses seen in the background are those in the Hemplands and Osborne Street, the latter now sliced in two by Jubilee Way and no longer extending to the High Street.

Camden Street, May 1990. Even before the incursion of Jubilee Way, Camden Street was one of the shortest streets in the town. Situated next to the High Street filling station, these houses were all that survived out of a terrace of six. A street map of about 1904 makes the interesting supposition that possibly Camden Street might have linked Melbourne Road with the High Street at some future date.

This photograph was taken from approximately the same position today, but nothing apart from the road sign suggests that we are even looking at the same place. The filling station now covers the whole of the area from Belle Vue Close to Camden Street, supplying petrol to traffic travelling both to and from Great Yarmouth.

The upper part of the High Street, *c.* 1897. This gives a good impression of the narrowness of the street prior to widening. Both sides dated back at least three centuries, although the tall building in the centre, the Rectory, was built in 1870. In the distance is Arnold House, then still in the Arnold family. J Rand, a local postman, lived not far away at 26 High Street: could he be the postman pictured here?

The upper part of the High Street today still bears the scars of the Fokker Wulfe raid on the town in May 1943, when many of those premises on the cliff side were destroyed. A few opposite were also badly damaged. Arnold House survived, and is remembered as the home of Jack Cleveland, a well-respected local benefactor. Now converted into flats, it overlooks the gardens laid out as a memorial to the raid.

High Street, September 1949. The fence on the left marks the site of the buildings destroyed in May 1943. The ruins of the 'Candy Store', partly hidden behind an advertising hoarding, indicates its antiquity. Like many buildings in the street, it possessed an earlier structure under its Georgian or Victorian frontage. Gaskin's (centre), with the overhanging first storey, hides even earlier, fifteenth-century, work. (*Waveney District Council*)

The 'Candy Store' and its hoarding have long gone, showing the side of 26 High Street, now part of the North Flint House, through the trees. There are gardens where there was once wasteland over fifty years before, and the main trunk road turns right into Camden Street. Only buses and cycles are allowed to continue down the High Street from this point.

East Holme, 27 High Street, *c.* 1908. Dating from the sixteenth century, it had links with the Mighells and Ashbys, and the naval wars of the seventeenth and eighteenth centuries. It became the town's vicarage on the death of John Arrow in 1789. A girl's school in the early years of the twentieth century, it was given to the town around the end of the Second World War.

It was hoped that the North Flint House, as it became known, would become the town's museum; however, it was used as the public library until 1951, and then as borough offices. Sold off in the early 1960s, it and the house to its left became firstly a restaurant and a night club, and then a public house. From that point it was a downhill journey, and at the time of writing (July 2000) it stands empty waiting for a buyer.

John Leslie stands in the doorway of Leslie's Outfitters, 165 High Street, *c.* 1938. A travelling draper in Chapel Street from around 1908 to the early 1930s, Leslie had moved to Sussex Road by 1934 before opening his shop in the High Street. Tobacconist Alfred Taylor is on the left. The ornate street-light in the foreground once supplied power to the town's trams.

Today a doorway marks 165 High Street, now part of Albany House, a large block of flats. Until the mid-1990s, it was part of Suffolk Water, also known as the post-war headquarters of the Lowestoft Water & Gas Company. The alleyway to the right leads to Albany Road. 'Sgt Pepper's' (right) is one of many restaurants in this area.

White Horse Street, *c*. 1960. Part of the clearances of the early 1960s, this photograph was taken from the corner of Compass Street looking towards the Morning Star public house in Mariners Street and the bottom of the Hemplands. Walter Emery's is the shuttered shop with the gas lamp. The shadow on the road belongs to W.B. Cooper's warehouse. (*Ray Vincent – Studio 161*)

The shadow of Cooper's old warehouse, now Waveney District Council offices, is still there today. Now, however, it reaches across Jubilee Way. The flats, built in the 1960s, stretch across the western part of Mariner's Street, finally cleared of old buildings in the early 1970s. In the distance are the remaining houses of the Hemplands, with Osborne Street beyond.

The Town Hall, *c.* 1896. This is the historic centre of the old town; the view shows all too clearly the narrowness of the upper part of the old High Street. Many buildings had been erected on pre-Dissolution foundations with later fronts hiding Tudor and Stuart interiors. The Town Hall itself was built in 1857 on the site of the old Corn Cross and Town Chamber erected in 1698. Also seen here are the Star of Hope and the Red Lion in Compass Street, two of the many public houses surrounding the Town Hall. Needless to say, Lowestoft's first mayor, William Youngman, was a brewer. In front of the Red Lion, where the two girls are standing, was the town's market-place from 1853 until its removal at the end of the nineteenth century to what later became the Triangle market. Note the long line of the roof of the town chamber on the upper floor of the Town Hall.

The scene today emphasises the difference street widening made at the beginning of the twentieth century. The public houses were swept away and in later years the old market-place became a car park. The front of the Town Hall, rebuilt between 1899 and 1900, still retains some feel of the earlier Italianate tower while the rear of the building remains the late 1850s original. No longer the hallowed corridors of the Borough Corporation, since the boundary changes of 1974 it is now the main offices of Waveney District Council. However, it retains close links with Lowestoft's historic past. The curfew bell, made in 1644 from brass taken from St Margaret's Church and recast in the eighteenth century, still rings out at 8 pm – although for how long depends on the clock mechanism which is now starting to show its age. On the right a block of modern shops, the aftermath of the last war, is an interloper on the corner of Mariner's Score.

Nothing was more devastating to the history of the town than the destruction of Duke's Head Street, seen here in 1960. This study by Norman Briggs LRPS, viewed from the High Street, shows this once important thoroughfare at the end of its long life. Originally named after the Old Blue Anchor public house, in the nineteenth century the street was renamed after another public house in the vicinity, the Duke's Head, long gone by the date of the photograph. John Wesley preached here between 1764 and 1790. Percy Wigg's furniture shop is on the corner next to the limited waiting sign. The road between Wigg's and the

shuttered Greyhound public house led to Old Market Plain. On the same side was Cleveland's secondhand shop and Bushell's Bakery, a family business going back to 1883. At the top of the thoroughfare was Chapel Street. On the right, the north side of Duke's Head Street, Mrs Baker's wardrobe shop stood on the corner of Gun Lane. Several wells or pumps were once to be found in the area. One was in Denny's Yard, between Norman Smith's Good Companions snack bar – where the bikes are parked – and Kirby's boot and shoe repair shop.

Gun Lane, 1983. At least in name, anyway. After the construction of Manor Court (left), Gun Lane was moved nearer to the High Street. The original lane led to White Horse Street and Chapel Street; now, however, it joins Wesleyan Chapel Lane. The old chapel in the High Street, built in 1862, once seated 900 but had become derelict by the 1980s after a period as a warehouse.

A sheltered housing complex was built on the site of the old Wesleyan chapel after its demolition in 1984. At one time it looked as if Wesleyan Chapel Lane itself would also disappear. Today's scene is dominated by the car park in the foreground, laid out on the south side of Duke's Head Street and also covering what had once been Old Market Plain, now under Artillery Way.

Entrance to the original Gun Lane, Duke's Head Street, *c*. 1904. Long before Mrs Baker had her wardrobe shop there, gasfitter George Leech could be found announcing 'Chimneys and flue cleaners – 6*d*'. The face of a little boy, possibly his son, stares through the glass in the door at the camera.

Demolition of Duke's Head Street, 1963. Since 1959 relics of the town's past, some dating back to the seventeenth century, if not earlier, had been swept away in the zeal to rid the town of what by then had become unhealthy slums. Eventually a complete chapter of the town's history disappeared under the hammers of the demolition gang. (*I.J. Mitchell*)

Modern Duke's Head Street from the High Street. Little survives of the old thoroughfare: St Peter's Court, built in the 1960s and Lowestoft's only high-rise block of flats, dominates the scene. One consolation during the demolition and rebuilding was the discovery of material from the old china factory in Factory Street. Percy Wigg's is now a restaurant; the old snack bar (centre) closed in 1995.

Jubilee Way today, looking north towards the Hemplands, across what was once the junction of Chapel Street and the western end of Duke's Head Street. Much is now taken up by the roundabout in the foreground, part of the main A12 trunk road. The only remnant of the past visible in this scene, Cooper's old warehouse (centre left), is now district council offices.

High Street looking towards greengrocer Percy Coleby's shop (centre) and the junction of Duke's Head Street, February 1977. Although the building on the corner is older, it had a pair of unique doors dating back to when the shop was a butcher's in the 1860s. A fruiterer's by 1900, it was taken over by Coleby in the 1930s, who continued the business until the end of the 1970s.

Through the High Street regeneration scheme, many buildings are now being restored, giving them a new lease of life. What was once Coleby's underwent much-needed renovation earlier this year (2000), but the most noticeable change in the High Street occurred in 1997 with the Triangle Area Improvement Scheme, pedestrianising much of the street southwards from Duke's Head Street.

The Triangle market-place from the High Street looking towards the junction with St Peter's Street, summer 1989. Removed from Compass Street, a site it had used since the 1850s, the town's market was relocated on land originally proposed for a new town hall. However, the new site proved popular and the market remained here for around a century. Fighting off competition in the late 1980s from the Britten Centre, the opening of Artillery Way in 1994 (cutting off the High Street from London Road North, the town's commercial centre) sounded its death knell. Shops in the area as well as the market itself soon fell into decline. The post-war market stalls seen here survived until 1996. Connaught House, second left from Michael Wood's turf accountants, was built in 1814. It was a Church Home for Girls in the 1890s, and by the early 1900s became a Home for Waifs and Strays. It is best remembered, however, as the town's School Clinic.

Surrounded by over 300 years of history, the Triangle market has been revitalised by both Waveney District Council and the European Community. The European Regional Development Fund has brought a new lease of life to the area. The market-place, now moved nearer to Artillery Way, boasts not only its regular Friday market but also special events and themed markets throughout the year.

The market's old site, now reduced in size, remains earmarked for redevelopment. Meanwhile, it is used as an extension to weekend events in the Triangle – here, for instance, the annual vintage vehicle rally. This brings out the exhibits from the East Anglian Transport Museum, including poignant reminders of the workmanship of the Eastern Coachworks factory.

A bomb-damaged Camp's Antiques separates Old Nelson Street (left) from London Road North, February 1949. The Albion Stores, in the 1860s the Ship public house, boasted it was 'the most easterly pub in England' after the clearing of the Beach Village in the 1960s. Stead & Simpson, next to Easiphit, would reopen in the early 1950s. (*Waveney District Council*)

The same scene today – the result of the Triangle Area Improvement Scheme. The pedestrianised area, with its vibrant Friday market and variety of shops, attracts visitors throughout the year. The Albion became the Larder Café in the 1980s; Studio 161 is next door. Easiphit is now a charity shop, and its boarded up neighbour of 1949 is The Crossing. Artillery Way cuts across all; the archway is in London Road North.

Where the High Street once met London Road North, June 1987. Sniffers and Proteus are in the High Street while Cook's furnishers marks the start of London Road North on the left. The view is taken from Old Nelson Street, before the London toll-road in the 1790s, the continuation of the road south to Ipswich. The car on the right is coming out of Barnard's Yard.

Artillery Way, the eastern relief road, now cuts through what had been Sniffers and Proteus – showing clearly how effectively the High Street is severed from the town centre. It also takes a chunk out of Arnold Street. Although doing nothing to improve matters for traffic travelling towards the Bridge, Artillery Way has, admittedly, made it easier for heavy traffic to get to and from the Whapload Road industrial estate.

Old Nelson Street, *c.* 1911. This once led down from the High Street to the South Beach, as it was known in the days of the eighteenth-century resort. In the distance beyond Battery Green the sea once lapped upon sandy shores, and the gentry took to the waters. The old houses (centre) may have dated back to Stuart times. Most shown here were destroyed during the last war.

History repeats itself and Old Nelson Street today is once more the main route to London. After the war a rebuilding programme was started on the eastern side but never continued. What was there, both old and new, was eventually swept away in the 1970s to make way for the present police station, joined in the late 1980s by a new magistrates' court. The top of the street became part of Artillery Way.

Bow House, Old Nelson Street, 1976. One of the few houses on the eastern side to survive the war-time carnage of Old Nelson Street, this unique corner house dated back to the eighteenth-century resort and was used as a public house by soldiers manning the South Battery opposite on the Battery Green, the largest of three batteries erected in 1782 to defend the town against French invasion.

Modern Old Nelson Street leads to a different scene. Before it was swept away, Bow House would have been near the car behind the road sign (centre). Battery Green itself gave way to a large roundabout and Lowestoft's first multi-storey car park. Christ Church's steeple marks the Denes industrial estate. Ness Point is behind the gasworks.

Old Nelson Street, 1960s. A cyclist travelling up towards the High Street passes cottages that were old even a hundred years before. Many of these dwellings witnessed the heyday of the town's first South Beach with its bathing huts introduced in the 1760s, allowing the fashionable, who may have lodged or rented houses similar to the one in the distance, to bathe in private. (*Ray Vincent – Studio 161*)

Today's view of what was the foot of Old Nelson Street, seen from Hamilton Road, looks across to Nelson Court, which was built in the late 1990s. Those old houses of the 1960s are under a car park and almost nothing now survives of Lowestoft's early resort.

CHAPTER TWO

LONDON ROAD NORTH

Stangroom's, 121 London Road North, 1977. Tucked between Taylor's newsagents and Leatherluxe, it had been the surgery of Dr Claud Ticehurst before the last war before becoming Stangroom's estate agents. This and several neighbouring properties were cleared to make way for Tesco's supermarket expansion in the late 1970s.

Eldrick Norton's, tobacconists and dealers in glass and chinaware, 163 & 165 London Road North, December 1979. One old sign remained on the shop, old fashioned by the 1970s but sought after by collectors – an empty space indicates at least one sign had already gone. Chapman & Utting's ornate entrance on the right once led to W.J. Balls' auction rooms. Tom Balls had been the auctioneer at the sale of the Sparrow's Nest estate at the Public Hall in 1897. Mr Borwick of Borwick baking powder fame was looking for a summer retreat in the area. Bidding therefore was fierce. Eventually the estate was sold to Lowestoft Corporation for just over £7,000.

Now part of Lloyds TSB bank next door, the ground floor and interior were completely altered after the bank's expansion into Norton's old shop. However, the original façade remained on the upper two storeys and, like the windows, is still recognisable today. Before renumbering in the 1880s, 163 and 165 London Road North had been numbered from the High Street end as nos 14 and 13 respectively. Jonathan Redgrave had been a corn-chandler at no. 13 in the 1860s. By the early 1880s Ernest Newton was running his tobacconist's there. The 1880s also saw watchmaker and jeweller F. Money at no. 14. The Refuge Assurance office – no. 12 in those early days – was taken over some years ago.

London Road North, 1954. The scars of war are still in evidence: the open space on the left where Rogers once stood, the Central Methodist church with its damaged steeple, and behind the bus stop (right) the Arcade site where Perrédès the chemists, Lowestoft Water & Gas and the Arcade itself once stood. This is also a rare record of Morling's temporary music shop (left). (*Waveney District Council*)

Trees and flower beds decorate the street where the photographer stood in 1954. The Arcade site became the Cooperative Stores in 1963, later changing its name to Westgates. Most of the rebuilding from Regent Road to Milton Road was completed by 1964; the opposite side was finished at about the same date.

Parasols on the upper deck of a Corporation tram on a summer's day in London Road North, *c.* 1910. The tram is the only mechanical vehicle in sight, although a shop on the left is advertising motors and cycles. H.G. Rogers, stationers and fine art depot (right), were the publishers of this particular view. At the top of the road is the High Street. (*Ray Vincent – Studio 161*)

This part of London Road North bears no comparison today with its Edwardian self. Where trams once travelled is now a pedestrian area. The ferocity of the last war left this area as part of the largest open space in Lowestoft. H.G. Rogers moved to the High Street. Only the Halifax Building Society and watchmaker and jeweller P.J. Gillman returned to their pre-war addresses, albeit to new buildings.

The Falcon public house in Police Station Road, seen here in 1977, was the last of the surviving buildings bearing witness to the destruction of the Arcade site during the last war. It was reopened in the 1950s and continued at least to the early 1960s, but by the 1970s it was used solely for storage. The tall mast is on the roof of Morling's House of Music at 149–51 London Road North.

The Falcon had gone by mid-1980. All that is now left is an empty space at the rear of the shops in London Road North used for parking. Today nothing earlier than the mid-1950s survives between Milton Road East and Regent Road. Morling's well-known radio mast has also gone, superseded by a satellite dish.

The junction of Milton Road looking towards the Falcon in Police Station Road, *c.* 1954. Bombed-out ruins of shops in London Road North could still be seen. Apart from the Falcon, two small premises just inside Milton Road managed to get through the war comparatively unscathed. One, Lane's sweet shop, was the first stop for parents visiting their children at the hospital. (*Waveney District Council*)

The view from the junction with Milton Road, now Milton Road East, looks very different today. Lane's sweet shop went in the early 1960s. Wholesalers Henry Pike rebuilt their premises on the corner of Police Station Road, in later years an office equipment centre; and on the left, near where the ruins once stood, is a home improvement showroom, originally Porter's motor-cycles.

Marine Terrace, September 1949. Treasure House Antiques, the ornate house at the end of the terrace (centre left), displays its cases of bric-a-brac – which hide part of Doreen's the florists (centre). The art-deco premises on the right were the Borough electricity showrooms, built on the site of London Road North Council School. (*Waveney District Council*)

Despite many changes, a taxi rank for instance, this area still retains a feel of its early post-war period although Doreen's has long gone, replaced by a clothes shop, and the electricity showrooms have been totally rebuilt. The house with the ornate doorway remains; it was once the home of architect W. Oldham Chambers who in the late nineteenth century designed this and many other buildings in Lowestoft.

Shops between Gordon Road and Regent Road await their fate in 1977. Demolished to make way for Tesco's supermarket expansion, these had once been substantial houses in a leafy suburb, only to become commercial properties by the 1920s. Facing Doreen's and the Eastern Electricity showrooms, Tesco's arrived in Lowestoft in 1964, opening on what had previously been Curtiss' Restaurant.

The red-brick façade of Tesco's modern town centre supermarket spans the width where most of those houses once stood. This area is also one of only two in London Road North which have not been pedestrianised, and is used for bus routes travelling to and from the northern parts of the town. It includes the bus stop still remembered as 'the Arcade', moved in the 1980s from outside the *Journal* office.

Eastern Counties garage and bus station, Gordon Road, 1985. Just off London Road North, it was originally the Regent Alfresco Theatre, built in the grounds of a large house, and opened in about 1920 complete with gardens and a driveway. Eastern Counties subsequently took over the site in the 1930s, converting the theatre into garages and concreting the gardens.

The old theatre was swept away with the building of the Britten Centre. A large gap where goods are delivered to the shops in the Centre arcade marks where the theatre once stood. The bus station has been part of the Britten Centre complex since 1987 although the garage and workshops were moved down to the Denes. Eastern Counties became part of Firstbus after deregulation in the 1990s.

Catling's department store, late 1970s. Both the store and the Central Methodist church had been the only survivors in this part of the street following the Waller raid in January 1942. The church was demolished in 1956 and replaced by Milletts and Courts. Catling's itself went in 1980 when Fine Fare supermarket took over the premises.

Behind this façade is Somerfield, the descendant of that Fine Fare store. Built on the Catling's site in 1983, it also contains Lowestoft's first multi-storey car park at the rear. This, the northern reaches of the main pedestrianised area, was constructed at about the same time as the supermarket.

The Odeon Cinema, 1979. Opened in January 1937 amid great ceremony by the mayor of Lowestoft, Selwyn Humphrey, with the band of the 2nd Battalion Lancashire Fusiliers supplying the music, it was built on the site of Chipperfield's the ironmongers. The premier cinema of the town, it took on a very different role during the Second World War when in January 1942, and although badly damaged itself, it acted as a mortuary for many of the dead in the aftermath of the Waller raid. Following the advent of television, the Odeon fell on mixed fortunes, like many cinemas throughout the country, and finally closed its doors in April 1979. The vacant shop between the Odeon and Freeman, Hardy & Willis had been Alexandre's outfitters not long before this photograph was taken. The Prairie separates the Odeon and Paige's dress shop.

The Odeon site was cleared for a new W.H. Smith store. Paige's, with Bata's next door, was also to disappear with the arrival of Dorothy Perkins in the mid-1980s, but the most significant change was the Britten Centre, opened in November 1987 by actor Peter Davison, then at the height of his fame as Doctor Who. In the midst of the town centre, this striking W.H. Smith store and the entrance to the Britten Centre leads people into the first shopping arcade in Lowestoft since the loss of the Victoria Arcade during the Second World War. The Britten Centre is built on a grander scale than its predecessor. Its centrepiece is the parade of shops in what is still officially the Prairie and leads to the Centre's own market – the town's main market-place since the opening of Artillery Way.

The roof of Gordon Road bus station looks over to the Prairie in 1985, marking the end of what was once part of an estate on the west side of the London toll-road. Although small, many of these were at one time boarding houses, but by the 1970s the area had become rundown.

The heart of the Britten Centre arcade today. The Prairie survives as the Centre's promenade where people sit and rest after a hard day's shopping or just idly watch the passing crowds. From this point they can also easily reach the Public Library, the Centre's market-place and Gordon Road bus station.

London Road North, *c.* 1912. This was the embryo of the later town centre; on the left are houses slowly being turned into shops – like Johnson Brothers, which survived until the 1950s. They are quite a contrast with those opposite. Waller's restaurant (centre right) has the blind with the refreshments sign. The trees belong to the Baptist church, opened in 1899. (*Ray Vincent – Studio 161*)

Astounding changes have happened over the years, brought on by war and pedestrianisation. Once, people crossing from side to side had to vie with traffic; today it is street furniture. Underneath many of the modern shops on the left are signs of those earlier houses, albeit long stripped of their gardens.

Waller's restaurant and café, a typical art-deco shop of the period, late 1930s. Two female assistants (left) look out of windows that reflect the shops opposite, among them the distinctive shape of Craik's fruiterers and confectioners, and Freeman, Hardy & Willis' shoe shop. Cakes from a penny to a shilling and Black Magic chocolates at 2s 10d a box are part of the display. In the midst of the town's shopping centre, Waller's restaurant and café was a favourite meeting place until the early years of the Second World War. On the afternoon of Tuesday 13 January 1942 a low-flying Dornier aircraft came in from the sea and dropped four high-explosive bombs on the town centre. Shops and businesses on both sides of the Marina were destroyed. Almost a complete block was razed to the ground. Waller's, at the time full with civilian and military personnel, received a direct hit. Most of the 70 deaths and 143 injuries occurred here. Many surrounding buildings were severely damaged. It took over four days to dig out survivors.

Opposite: The shops were rebuilt in the early 1950s. Waller's themselves moved further along London Road North. Within the last five years the block has been refaced, and in recent months the plot where Waller's had been before the war was being refitted into one large unit.

Although Waller's was completely destroyed, the shops opposite survived the war. Wimpy's fast food restaurant now takes the place of Craik's, which closed in the late 1960s. Freeman, Hardy & Willis also survived the war and continued for many years before becoming the Abbey National Building Society and Rachel James.

Suffolk Hotel, *c.* 1860. Originally a coaching inn, Robert Clarke was mine host at the date of this photograph. A popular meeting place, behind the flintstone wall was a green kept by Mr Clarke for the recreation of his clientele. The arrival of the railway in Lowestoft in 1847 meant that the old hotel soon became too small, and in 1873 a much larger Suffolk Hotel was built. (*Mrs J. Plant*)

McDonald's is now on the site of both the old and the later Suffolk Hotel. Built in 1974, it was Lipton's supermarket until the early 1980s. Now mainly pedestrianised, this part of London Road North, like so much of the street, has changed dramatically, especially since Mr Clarke's day when the London to Yarmouth coach would thunder across the bridge towards the Suffolk Hotel.

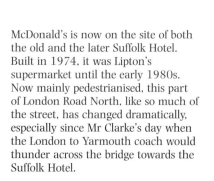

NORTH LOWESTOFT

Once part of J.W. Brooke's Adrian Works in Alexandra Road, this
photograph taken in the mid-1980s shows the old workshop
being used by Court's as a furniture warehouse: the circular
window over the entrance is synonymous with the work of local
architect W.J. Roberts in the 1890s. The building was demolished
in the late 1990s.

Empty shops on the corner of Raglan Street on the left, and Bevan Street await their fate in May 1976, prior to the construction of Katwijk Way, the southern part of the North Lowestoft spinal relief road. The new road would cut through the shops nearest to the camera and take the east side of Raglan Street up to Till Road. Note the half-hidden small modern shop (centre right).

NO PARKING

Once inconspicuously tucked away in among many, this shop – now in Bevan Street East – looks across to the houses opposite in Bevan Street West from where this photograph was taken. Trees and shrubs hide Katwijk Way, which severed much of Bevan Street (at this point mainly houses) from the town centre.

Katwijk Way under construction in the summer of 1977. The new road also had a drastic effect on Tonning Street (right), a busy thoroughfare for some one hundred years. Although the wall seen here acted as sound-proofing, cutting down the noise of traffic using the new road, it also helped to cut Tonning Street off from the town centre. St John's steeple peers over the roofs of Commercial Road.

Katwijk Way today. A sharp turn at the lights outside the railway station in Denmark Road, towards the camera, leads traffic past London Road North and towards St Peter's Street. Seen here from the first of two crossings linking the adjoining residential areas to the town centre, the slip-road on the left leads to the shops in Bevan Street East. Tonning Street is on the right.

The Wesleyan chapel and Sunday school, not long after its opening in 1866. It was situated on the corner of Tonning Street and Flensburgh Street, two of the streets laid out for the men and their families working in the new port and fish market of Lowestoft. Over the years several local business families had links with the chapel, among them Bilverstones, Wiggs and Morlings. (*Richard Morling*)

Chadds used the old chapel as a warehouse for some years before it was demolished in 1996. Houses are now to be found on the corner of Flensburgh Street and Tonning Street, their backways designed to cope with the modern problem of residential car parking.

The north side of Tonning Street, *c.* 1912. By this date the street had become a prosperous suburban thoroughfare, supporting a public house with two others close at hand, and also boasting a multitude of trades as well as a number of small shops that thrived in a community ranging from boarding houses to artisans' cottages. (*Ray Vincent – Studio 161*)

Tonning Street West, as it is known today, is mainly a residential area. Katwijk Way not only caused many of its shops to close, but was responsible for the demolition of Hughes TV, as well as the loss of the Stone Cottage public house. A dog parlour now takes the place of the printers of around 1912 – for many years Cook's the fishmongers.

The Ideal Cinema, on the corner of Union Road and Norwich Road, 1990. Derelict for many years, it was originally opened in 1936 by Alfred Maquire, but closed because of the war. It never reopened and over the intervening years the building went through a variety of uses. The remains of the sign over the entrance could be seen as late as the 1960s.

A semi-detached pair of houses built in the late 1990s is now on the site of the old cinema. Over the last decade there has been an increasing number of new homes built in and around Norwich Road. The old cinema and Stanley Street are among the sites that have been reused in the area.

Rear gardens on the east side of Clemence Street, 25 March 1916. Named after John Louth Clemence and located off Norwich Road, these artisan cottages were among a number of buildings damaged when a German cruiser squadron opened fire on the resort in the early morning of Tuesday 25 April 1916. Four people were killed, three in Sandringham Road not far from Clemence Street.

East side of Clemence Street, 2000. The backyards of those houses bombed in Clemence Street during the First World War have changed beyond recognition. The low wooden fencing has long given way to tall brick walls. It is now difficult to say for sure, but these dwellings near the corner with Norwich Road may have been some of those shelled in 1916.

Edgar Bobbin's, butcher, Clapham Road, 1976. On the corner with Milton Road, the shop disappeared when much of the east side of Clapham Road was demolished for Katwijk Way. Milton Road itself was said to be part of an ancient route between Oulton Broad and the town dating back over a thousand years.

The entrance to Milton Road East from Katwijk Way now sits where Bobbin's shop could once be found. The backs of the houses on the right are those in Regent Road. The wall in the foreground separates Katwijk Way from Clapham Road, now a narrow residential street.

Victoria Dairy, Clapham Road, May 1976. The home of Ada Roe, at one time Britain's oldest shopkeeper, who died in January 1970 not long before her 112th birthday. Born in London, she moved to Lowestoft for her husband's health and here they opened the dairy. The empty space on the right had been the Anchor Garage. The backyards are those in Leiston Road.

The only thing left is the entrance to the alleyway on the right, which was once between the shop and the garage. It leads to the rear of Leiston Road and towards Alexandra Road. Behind the modern wall is a car park hidden in front of the Anchor smokehouse, one of the few smokehouses left in the town, a remnant of Lowestoft's famed herring industry. Katwijk Way is in the foreground.

The demolition of Adrian Works, Alexandra Road, May 1990. When J.W. Brooke built his workshop on the Ten Acre Field in the 1870s, it was at the edge of the town. Founded in 1873, Brooke's moved into car production in 1902 – their most famous vehicle being the swan-bodied car built in 1912. After the last war East Anglian Engineering and later Swallow Prams were here for some years.

Alexandra Road Surgery moved here from Gordon Road in the early 1990s. Also on the site of the old Brooke workshops is a sheltered housing complex. Fortunately not all the old buildings were pulled down: the Adrian Works offices survived (visible in the distance) and are now part of Suffolk County Council education offices.

The east side of Arnold Street, 1993. Although not far from the town centre, Arnold Street was almost a community in its own right. The Infants' School building (centre), erected in 1884, survived until the early 1990s, albeit as car sales and repairs. The old drill hall (right), once used by the Artillery Volunteers, still sported its unique façade. A garage by the 1920s, it was also being used for car repairs and sales.

Arnold Street is now a cul-de-sac, closed off at its uppermost end with the building of Artillery Way. All on the east side from the old drill hall up to St Peter's Street disappeared later in 1993 with the construction of the new road, which was named in honour of Arnold Street's old drill hall. The façade of the old hall survives, although the building itself was shortened.

The old steam flour mill at the top of Arnold Street, 1979. This is almost as it might have appeared when Campbell & Witham had the mill from the 1920s to the late 1950s. In later years it became Godfrey's warehouse. The sports car seen here is parked outside what was once the mill house (left).

A substantial structure, the mill and some of its outbuildings survive today as part of a residential complex built in the mid-1990s. The tall chimney went in the last decade, as did Davy's yard and the small lock-up next door. The mill house itself, however, still survives. On the other side of the wall on the right is the junction of Artillery Way with St Peter's Street.

Dove Street from St Margaret's Plain, early 1976. Dwarfed by St Peter's Court in the background, these ancient dwellings were what was left of the street apart from a handful of buildings to the left out of camera range. They had been in a derelict state for some time when this photograph was taken. The backways, roofs and chimneys belong to Crown Street West.

The site seen today from the purpose-built car park on St Margaret's Plain is identified only by the tall fencing posts next to one of the few houses left in Dove Street. The boarded-up house in the centre in 1976 was demolished a decade later, while the derelict shop and its store were used for a while for tyres until destroyed by fire in the 1990s.

The front of Boston Lodge, *c.* 1908. It was the French Convent Boarding School for Young Ladies at this date. George Shadworth, mayor of Lowestoft from 1929 to 1931, lived here in the 1920s. Part of the lodge grounds became Beaconsfield Bowling Green by the 1930s, but the lodge itself is best remembered as the North Lowestoft Youth Club of the 1950s.

Boston Lodge Youth Centre now stands in what is left of the grounds of the old lodge, demolished in the 1960s when Boston Road itself was improved. Not much of the original site survives; the old flintstone boundary wall went with the paving of this side of Boston Road. Where the house once stood (right) is now a fenced ball area.

A cottage on the corner of Crown Street and Boston Road, 1880s. Overlooking the Three-cornered Green at the junction of Boston Road, Beccles Road and St Peter's Street, this small cottage was almost in the country, despite being only ten minutes' walk away from the High Street. The woman and the girl may have known the photographer, John Barrett, who lived not far away in Church Road.

No trace of the cottage will be found on the corner of today's Crown Street West. It was located between the house on the corner and the traffic island marking the junction of Crown Street West with Boston Road. Even the remnants of the Green, parts of which survived until the early 1970s, have gone. In the distance is the First and Last public house.

Lowestoft Convalescent Home, Fairfield House, *c.* 1880. Opened in 1877 on what was then known as the Belle Vue Estate, it was enlarged in 1882 at a cost of £2,000. It was, as *White's Directory* described it, 'for those likely to benefit by sea bathing or a temporary residence by the seaside'. F.S. Worthington was medical advisor at the time and may be the man standing at the entrance on the left.

Trinity Methodist church, opened in 1970, now stands in front of the old house, known today as Abigail Court. The house itself is seen here from the car park in Park Road with what had been the Convalescent Home chapel nearest to the camera. The grounds also include the High Street Surgery.

Park-keeper's lodge, Belle Vue Park, *c.* 1920. Situated opposite the Convalescent Home on what was once common land, the park includes the site of the North Battery of the 1780s. Planned for pleasure grounds as early as 1814, it was only in 1874 that Belle Vue Park was eventually laid out. What may be a weather station can be seen between the group of visitors and the bandstand.

The Cottage was destroyed by fire in February 1990. However, plans were soon afoot to reconstruct it as faithfully as possible to the original. Finished in 1991, the rebuilt Cottage is just as impressive as its predecessor, and has become popular as a picturesque backdrop notably for wedding groups from the Trinity Methodist church opposite.

North Parade, looking across the Ravine from Belle Vue Park, mid-1890s. The two large houses were built in the 1860s; the rest followed by the early 1890s. The Ravine Bridge, designed by R. Parkinson, engineer to the Eastern & Midlands Railway, was presented to the town by Lowestoft's first mayor William Youngman in 1887 to celebrate Queen Victoria's Golden Jubilee.

The Jubilee Bridge still links the Belle Vue Park to the North Parade, now well hidden from view by over a century and a quarter's growth of trees and bushes, which are well nourished by the number of natural underground springs in the vicinity which tend periodically to seep through the joints in the concrete roadway.

Hollingsworth Road, looking towards Yarmouth Road, 1946. In 1944 Park Farm, Gunton, was acquired as part of the town's post-war rehousing programme. Many had returned from the war to bomb-damaged homes or moved in with in-laws. More than a few opted to live in converted sheds or carriages, but shortages of men and material meant that Gunton would take some four years to complete. (*Waveney District Council*)

The same block today with the tower of St Benedict's Church on the corner of Hollingsworth Road and Yarmouth Road. Originally called the Yarmouth Road Housing Site, apart from Spashett Road and Hollingsworth Road, all the thoroughfares on the Gunton Estate were named after wartime leaders, battles or the town's naval stations.

Foundations of houses in Tedder Road, *c*. 1947. They are seen from El Alamein Road, the highest point on the Gunton Estate, looking across to the roofs of many of its 350 prefabs. Shortage of wood had a serious effect on the construction of houses: these here, for instance, would take another year. Montgomery Avenue (right), begun in July 1946, was not yet finished. (*Waveney District Council*)

The houses in Tedder Road were eventually completed in about 1948. Today they are a combination of owner occupiers, council and housing association properties. The prefabs were demolished in the early 1960s. Although the road itself is not very wide, Tedder Road was once the terminus of the Corporation buses – now superseded by private cars.

Orlit houses, Minos Road, Gunton Estate, 1985. Because it was built as the result of the needs of the end of the war and never as a 'working-class' estate, houses in Gunton were of a high standard. This included the Orlit prefabricated houses erected in 1948 because of the urgent need for homes. They lasted longer than envisaged: it was nearly forty years before they were demolished.

Today only Mylodon Road in the distance and the lamp-post give some hint that this is Minos Road. The Orlits went in the late 1980s to be replaced by bungalows and family houses. Once the road was a haven for street games; now these modern houses are designed more to accommodate cars, to the detriment of gardens and play areas.

Rotterdam Cottages, Cemetery Road, *c.* 1900. They were situated on a road linking Rotterdam Road with St Margaret's Church. As far as can be ascertained, as the picture is faded, this view was taken before the construction of the Lowestoft to Yarmouth railway. The area was known as Rotterdam well before the nineteenth century, when a Rotterdam House was mentioned in the 1730s.

Now an extension of Rotterdam Road, a large roundabout stands where there was once a crossroads. St Margaret's Church, tall and proud on the horizon, indicates the highest point in Lowestoft. Council houses in Normanston Drive now face the corner where the cottages once stood. Hidden among the trees and hedges is the bridge over the now disused railway, which closed in about 1970.

Mortuary chapel, Lowestoft Cemetery, *c.* 1910. Fifteen acres of land had been laid out in 1885, with an extension added in 1903. The first person to be buried there was Mrs E. Rowe in February 1887. The Maconochie brothers, several members of the Capps family, as well as other notable fishing families, were all laid to rest here.

The trees have matured over the years and, like St Margaret's churchyard not far away, the cemetery has become a record of the people of the town. Of note are the graves of those who died in both world wars, and there is a poignant corner near Rotterdam Road itself where the final resting places can be found of some of those who were killed in the Waller raid of 1942.

Newson's Meadow nearing completion, *c.* 1937. Looking south from the top of the road towards St Peter's Street and the roofs of Minden Road (centre left), this addition to the Roman Hill Estate was located not far from the cemetery. Part of the town's housing improvement scheme, it was built on what had been George Newson's nursery. (*Waveney District Council*)

Despite being over sixty years old, Newson's Meadow still retains a vestige of its pre-war self, although the motor car has certainly made its presence felt. Trees have matured, double-glazing has replaced the old metal window frames, and the wooden fences of yesteryear have given way to brick walls.

Kent Road, 25 April 1916. Returning to the Rotterdam Road area, Kent Road is remembered for the naval attack in 1916 when a 12 in shell crashed through thirteen houses, finally landing in the last one without exploding. Nobody was killed or injured, which was a miracle in itself.

Three of the children in 1916 were playing outside these houses, seen some eighty-three years later. The small boy was standing outside the gate of the house whose door is hidden by the lamp-post in today's view. Although this is still a cul-de-sac, parked cars make street games, once an essential part of childhood, a thing of the past.

Eastern Coachworks, Eastern Way, January 1987. Opened in 1920 as the United Automobile Services coach-building factory in Laundry Lane, it began by building bus bodies for ex-military lorries. The company gradually expanded, and by the late 1920s it was building coach bodies for other operators. In 1936 it was renamed Eastern Coachworks and Laundry Lane became Eastern Way.

Eastern Coachworks closed in 1986. After some debate about its future, the factory was finally demolished in early 1989. Today Peto Way and the North Quay Retail Park, seen here, are on the site. Eastern Way itself remains – albeit in a truncated form – as a memorial to an industry that once made Lowestoft famous throughout the world.

CHAPTER FOUR
THE FISHING INDUSTRY

Unloading herrings, *c.* 1905. Lowestoft's reputation as a fishing town had already been established by the time the Fish Market opened in the 1850s. For centuries the town thrived on the herring and mackerel. Grandfathers, fathers and sons, as seen here, all earned their living from the sea.

Waveney Fish Dock, mid-1890s. Seen from the Mount, the lookout on the Trawl Market, the Dock had been opened in 1883 to cope with the increasing numbers of drifters using the port. In the foreground nets, boxes and barrels are being prepared for the next day's fishing. In the distance are houses and commercial properties on what, before 1885, had been the Grove Estate. (*Ann Hubbard*)

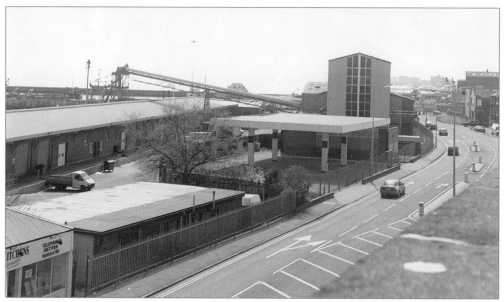

Looking from the multi-storey car park in Battery Green Road, today's view shows only the remnant of a once great industry. The Ice Company (centre right) still transports ice direct to vessels moored in the Herring Dock. The modern enclosed market, built in 1987, is a miniature of its old self. Kitchen showrooms replace ships' stores and a garage – at present closed – intrudes on the market itself.

LT 537 *Children's Friend*, *c.* 1935. Built in 1893 and seen here towards the end of its life, the smack was a type similar to those seen in the harbour on the previous page. By the early 1900s steam was taking over from sail, and by the 1930s most surviving smacks were run by owner/skippers. E.L. Hook and W.L. Pointer owned the *Children's Friend* at the date of this photograph.

LT 1005 *St Antony*, seen here in the Trawl Basin, is a typical modern Lowestoft fishing boat. New in 1999, she is one of a small number of vessels still working out of the port. Most of the companies that once owned fishing fleets have now diversified into other areas, and the once distinctive local trawler has long since given way to European-built vessels and different fishing techniques.

Trawl Dock, 1963. Among those here are trawlers from Small's, Boston and Colne Shipping Company, and include LT 130 *Grenada*, LT 361 *Grayfish* and LT 185 *Jamaica*. Railway trucks are still on the quayside next to the *Jamaica* (left), although by this date fish deliveries were mainly by road. The offices of Boston Deep Sea Fisheries, built in 1905, are on the corner of Waveney Road.

The old Trawl Market disappeared in about 1967. In its place Ross Group built a fish processing plant, itself demolished in the 1990s, leaving the site of the Trawl Market, seen here from Waveney Road, empty and barren. Between the railings and the rig, parked vans indicate where the Market, and in turn the processing plant, once were. At present the future of the port rests in the gas and oil industries.

Waveney Road, late 1960s. Home of the larger fishing companies, two of which are seen here – Small & Co. at Waveney Chambers, partly under scaffolding, and the Colne Shipping Company (right). Built on the old Grove Estate, this was the heart of Lowestoft's fishing industry. Concrete is being laid in the foreground as part of an improvement to the market. (*the late Ernest Graystone*)

Waveney Chambers no longer services the fishing industry, which has had to reduce its size and diversify into other spheres to survive. Small & Co. is now one of a number of businesses using the building, which also houses the *Lowestoft Journal*, having moved here from London Road North in 1998.

Explorator packing station, Battery Green Road, August 1963. Founded in 1947, Explorator pioneered the delivery of fish direct to the customer by refrigerated lorry. The packing station was situated almost opposite the entrance to the Fish Market. Danny Knights and Winky Norman are the two filleters on the left. Note the heater on the wall! (*the late Ernest Graystone*)

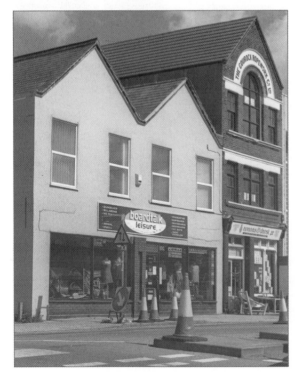

Boardtalk Leisure is now in what had been the Explorator packing station. Once split in two by a central stairway, filleters worked on the left while fish from the market was unloaded on the right. Both Boardtalk and Ananas & Dansk next door narrowly avoided destruction in 1999, when the Hippodrome Bingo Hall was destroyed in one of the biggest fires in the town since the war.

East Street, Beach Village, mid-1960s. Seen at the end of its life, the Beach was once inhabited mainly by fishermen and their families. Net stores, boat building and smokehouses also added to its character. However, there were problems – many properties were not in the best condition. The area had been declared a slum before the last war, but the final blow came with the Floods of 1953.

Newcombe Road is typical of the Beach today. East Street went with the demolition of the village in the 1960s and the area is now an industrial estate. Leading in from Hamilton Road, workshops, DIY stores and a variety of other businesses can be found, but very little – if anything at all – survives of the fishing.

Old net store, Whapload Road, late 1980s. Then in a fragile state, the flintwork on the end wall (right) suggested a date as early as the seventeenth century. Built in the days when fishing boats were dragged up on the beach and curing was done at the foot of the cliffs, it was believed to be the oldest example of its kind at the time of its collapse in 1989.

Although much of Lowestoft's fishing has gone, many of its traditions still carry on – for example this smokehouse in Raglan Street, where the tradition of smoking fish continues, not so much the herring, but nowadays cod, haddock and mackerel fillets. The pungent but pleasant aroma reminds us of a once great industry when herring was king, and Lowestoft herring in particular reigned supreme.

CHAPTER FIVE

SOUTH LOWESTOFT

Pier-master D. Carver (centre) with two attendants on the
South Pier, *c.* 1938. Behind them is the pavilion opened
in 1891. Holding the position of pier-master until 1940,
Mr Carver was responsible for many of the fishing
matches held on the pier during the 1930s. (*Mrs E. Hall*)

The Royal Hotel, *c.* 1864. Designed by John Thomas for Sir Morton Peto, it opened in 1849 and proved so successful that it was immediately enlarged. As *Hunt's Directory* for 1850 put it, it was 'for affording suitable accommodation for Families of Rank'. One of the town's naval land stations during the last war, the Royal unfortunately fell on difficult times in later years and was demolished in 1973.

The East Point Pavilion, opened in May 1993, was eventually built on the site. One of the original stone coats of arms that adorned the old hotel was placed in its information centre. For the best part of twenty years the site was part of Royal Green, a popular venue for events and displays. The kiosk on the left is part of the recently opened Adventure Golf Garden.

Two gentlemen halt before the camera between the Royal Mews and the Royal Hotel, 1890s. The long shadows suggest late afternoon. A booth (left) sells holiday wares. Also visible is the prefabricated headquarters of the Yacht Club (right). The Reeve monument on the Royal Plain, seen between the Yacht Club and the entrance to the Royal, was erected in 1891.

The Royal Mews, later to become the Palace Cinema, is now under a car park and the slip-road leading to Belvedere Road. The most significant building on the Royal Plain is the Royal Norfolk & Suffolk Yacht Club, opened in 1903. The Reeve monument went to Kensington Gardens in the 1920s, replaced by the present memorial dedicated to those who fell in the First World War. A dedication to those who died in the Second World War was added later.

The South Pier Pavilion, 1933. The second structure on the pier, it replaced the reading room burnt down in 1885. Parts of the original gateway to the pier were still there in the 1930s, by then joined by sideshows and kiosks. Jan Hurst with his Municipal Orchestra were at the South Pier that week; Reilly Comfort, Billy Hill and supporting cast were at the Sparrow's Nest.

Family entertainment is the order of the day at the entrance to today's South Pier. More colourful than its pre-war sibling, it is a complex where ten-pin bowling, bingo and children's games are all found under one roof – as well as fish and chips and, of course, Lowestoft Rock. Meanwhile, Triton still wrestles on his pedestal with his cornucopia, oblivious to the changes all about him.

South Pier Pavilion from the Fish Market, 1979. The old pavilion was demolished in 1954; a new one built in its place opened in 1956. The third and last pavilion to date, it was noted for its views of the town from its tower. Seen from the Trawl Market rebuilt in the 1960s, the pavilion was demolished between 1988 and 1989. Also here is LT 83 *St Nichola* moored in the Trawl Dock.

After nearly ten years as an empty plot, the pier became the home of Lowestoft's lifeboat crew with the erection of a new station in 1999 on the foundations of the Pavilion. Also near at hand in the Yacht Basin are seasonal attractions from Lowestoft's fishing past, the drifter *Lydia Eva* and the trawler *Mincarlo*. The pier meanwhile retains its popularity with anglers as a favourite spot to fish.

Nos 1 and 2 Esplanade after the German naval attack of 25 April 1916. The home of Lieutenant Colonel William Cadge before the First World War, it was situated next to the Royal Hotel which narrowly missed being hit. The view shows the initial damage caused by the shell when it struck the house.

A stroller rests on the Esplanade on a seat situated approximately in front of the grounds of those houses of 1916, now part of the Royal Green, and before that the putting green of the 1950s and 1960s. Marine Terrace, Pier Terrace and Royal Thoroughfare are in the background.

The Esplanade, 1959. Two world wars and a policy to demolish much of what was left to turn it into pleasure gardens found the seafront practically bereft of Peto's mansions. Seen here are 5, 6 and 7 Esplanade. Further along is no. 17, then St John's Vicarage. The miniature railway encircling the putting green survived until the early 1970s.

The view today from the new Adventure Golf Garden at the East Point Pavilion. The Millennium Beacon, the first in Britain to greet the new millennium, is centre left. St John's Vicarage of the 1950s, in the distance, is now one of the many amusement centres on the Esplanade.

Marine Parade, *c.* 1905. Designed by John Thomas, the terrace was built mainly as boarding houses for the new resort of south Lowestoft. At the beginning of the century luscious green ivy made for a pleasing thoroughfare in those days of horse-drawn traffic, and complemented the trees on the right in the rear gardens of the houses on the Esplanade. (*Ann Hubbard*)

The ivy has gone as have the houses on the Esplanade. The gentle jingling of horses pulling wagons loaded with holidaymakers has been superseded by the roar of traffic travelling south towards Ipswich and London. Apart from the parked cars, Marine Parade has survived surprisingly well, although flats have now taken the place of some of the boarding houses in the terrace.

St John's Church, London Road South, with Commercial Road in the distance, *c.* 1864. The church, designed by J.L. Clemence and then only ten years old, dominates an infant New Town Estate. Unmade pavements and vacant lots show building was still in progress. The flintstone walls on the right were made mainly of material gathered from local beaches. (*Ray Vincent – Studio 161*)

Today's view of London Road South is very different. Pier Terrace was built in the late 1860s. Hevingham House, behind the cinema sign, is on the site of the early rectory. St John's Church was demolished in 1978 and a sheltered housing complex, Levington House, was built in its place. The Hollywood Cinema itself is partly on the site of the right-hand house of the pair in the 1860s scene.

Primitive Methodist chapel, Mill Road, 1977. Designed in 1869 by W.O. Chambers, a local architect whose individualistic style can still be found throughout Lowestoft, it appears to be have been influenced by the work of Sir Morton Peto's architects John Thomas and J.L. Clemence. The building was used later as a garage and warehouse. In 1986 the chapel, as well as houses in Mill Road (left) and those on the corner of London Road South (right), were demolished to make way for a new Mann Egerton car showroom. At the time of the photograph the old chapel was used by a van-hire firm.

Mann Egerton garage, London Road South, *c.* 1936. An unnamed young lady and a group of mechanics pose on Mann Egerton's forecourt beside a Ford saloon car, about to venture on a seventy-two-hour non-stop trip, one of many such endurance tests held at the time – not bad for a new car costing just over £100. (*Ray Vincent – Studio 161*)

New Mann Egerton car showrooms were built in 1986. Known today as Waveney Rover, it is situated on the sites of the houses and chapel in Mill Road as well as Mann Egerton's old garage in London Road South. Over the years the block between Mill Road and Belvedere Road has lost many of its original buildings, many succumbing at one time or another to car showrooms.

Victoria Terrace, *c.* 1888. Mainly consisting of boarding houses and summer residences, it was in the centre of Peto's superior watering place. Adjacent to the grand and opulent Wellington Terrace, a mews housing horses and carriages of those staying for the season separated it from Marine Parade. To the left is South View in Wellington Road and the Victoria Hot & Cold Baths. (*Ray Vincent – Studio 161*)

Looking at Victoria Terrace today, South View in Wellington Road, now Waterloo Road, is one of the many buildings in Kirkley now being brought back to its former glory. Over the years the pale yellow brick had aged to a murky grey, but with the regeneration of Kirkley we can now see some of the splendours that were once part of the New Town.

Mrs Westgate and guests outside South View, Wellington Road, *c.* 1912. Seated resplendently among her guests with her pet dog in her lap, Mrs Westgate had run the boarding house since the 1880s. The children look ready to play on the South Beach once the photographer had finished, while their parents and older siblings strolled along the Esplanade; both were only minutes away.

Decorating the doorway behind Mrs Westgate's guests are these Arts and Crafts tiles dating from the 1860s, still to be found at the entrance of South View. These motifs are also repeated on the doorways of much of Victoria Terrace as well as some of the other houses in Waterloo Road.

Holidaymakers on the Esplanade, 1938. With visitors arriving on the Belle steamers, the Claremont Pier was a favourite spot with photographers. Father, mother with the obligatory box camera, and daughter are seen strolling past Wellington Gardens. The large building behind the young girl and featured in many of these photographs was at one time the Ministry of Agriculture, Fisheries and Foods.

That large building became the site for Peto House, seen here from Wellington Gardens, one of several sheltered homes in the area. The original was demolished in the 1950s and the vacant plot used as a car park for many years. The new building was designed in keeping with the re-emergence of interest in the work of Sir Samuel Morton Peto, and complements the surrounding locality.

The Claremont Pier, *c.* 1905. Built in 1903 as a staging post for the Belle steamers travelling to Great Yarmouth from London, like the South Pier it was a favourite haunt with anglers. At the entrance were the obligatory kiosks selling souvenirs. There were also opportunities to ride on the donkeys or be driven in one of the open carriages (bottom right).

An arcade of specially erected street lights leads from London Road South to the splendours of today's post-war Claremont Pier, at the time of this photograph undergoing preparations for the forthcoming season. Complementing the South Pier at the opposite end of the Esplanade, the Claremont also has a wide variety of entertainment including discos and bars.

The Esplanade, Kirkley Cliff and Wellington Terrace from Victoria Mansions, *c.* 1898. The view looks across to north Lowestoft from what fifty years before had been wasteland between the North Sea and Kirkley Ham. Even out of season there are still people taking the air along the spacious Esplanade. There are signs in Kirkley Cliff Road and Wellington Esplanade that a water sprayer has recently dampened down the dusty roads. South Lodge Preparatory School, famous for having Benjamin Britten as a pupil in the early 1920s, is in the centre of the scene. St John's spire peers over the roof-tops of Wellington Terrace (centre left). Garden plots or allotments are in the foreground. Considering its height, this photograph may have been taken while Victoria Mansions were still under construction.

Today's view, also taken out of season, shows how much development has taken place over the intervening years. Most noticeable is the loss of South Lodge, destroyed by fire some years after the school itself had moved to Old Buckenham in 1936. St John's steeple has also gone. The Thatched Restaurant and Coffee House, here since before the last war, Cliff Road and the car park in the foreground have taken the place of those plots seen years before. The Claremont Pier is on the right. It is a busy, popular resort, far outdoing Sir Samuel Morton Peto's original concept; today amusements and parks go hand in hand with promenades, boarding houses and beaches, and holidaymaker and local alike enjoy the spectacle of yacht and smack races, and the annual sea front air displays.

Kirkley church hall, *c.* 1883. The church hall was between St Peter's Church and Carlton Road; behind it can be seen the castellated edifice of Kirkley water tower, built across what would become St Peter's Road. Powered by steam, it had been supplying water to Kirkley for over forty years and predated Peto's New Town Estate. Judging by the gap in the fence, the church hall had been in use for some time.

Surrounded by early twentieth-century houses in what is now St Peter's Road, and with grounds extended to the front, today's church hall looks somewhat lost. Kirkley water tower has long since been demolished and replaced by houses in Carlton Road. Still used by the community of Kirkley, the church hall is also the headquarters of the 7th Lowestoft Scout Group.

CHAPTER SIX

PAKEFIELD

A small concerned group study the state of the cliff, Pakefield Street, *c.* 1930. Much of Pakefield's history has been a battle with the sea. A large proportion of the village had already disappeared by 1930, by which time much of Pakefield Street itself had also been lost.

Pakefield Street, c. 1920. The photograph looks inland towards London Road, Pakefield; at this date it was a stree still steeped in history. The Trowel and Hammer public house, the white building centre left, was one of the oldes surviving in the street. However, most of the others behind the photographer had gone – swept away by the sea Most of the properties on the right survived the peril – some only just. It is also worth comparing the two sides c the street. On the left is the village of Pakefield, outside the Borough boundary and still very much in the Victoria era. The right-hand side is in the Borough of Lowestoft – paved and in a comparatively good order. After the Firs World War most of the cliff erosion was on the village side, south of Pakefield Street. In Pakefield's case, th problem was that it did not become part of Lowestoft until 1934, by then too late for much of the village. Even th Jubilee Wall erected in 1936 could do little to help. (*Ray Vincent – Studio 161*)

With the exception of those nearest to the camera, most of those houses on the left in the previous scene have survived to the present time. There is a gap where the house with the bay window over the porch once stood: the owners possibly fearing the worst, this old house may have been demolished. Down the road, opposite the row of parked cars, can still be found the Trowel and Hammer, the same old inn little changed from the earlier photograph. Helped by the Jubilee Sea Wall of the 1930s and also with the build-up of the beach in front of the church over the past forty years or so, the danger of the rest of the village crashing into the sea has been averted for, we hope, a long time to come.

Beach Street, *c.* 1913. South of Pakefield Street, the cliff to the right shows the havoc being reeked by the sea cutting deep into Pakefield, turning what had been a substantial community into a small village. The houses and outbuildings hang on the cliff top waiting for their fate: the tide at the foot indicates that that was not long in coming. (*Ray Vincent – Studio 161*)

As can be imagined, locating the lost streets of Pakefield can have its difficulties, especially as some are now out to sea – but as far as can be ascertained, Beach Street may have been in the area of what is now the eastern extension of All Saints Road, seen here from the cliff edge not far from Kirkdale Court.

All Saints' and St Margaret's Church, 1920s. Technically two churches, the result of rival claims to the manor of Pakefield, it was not until 1746 that both parts were officially under one rector. Once some distance inland, by the 1920s the sea was beginning to threaten the area in front of the church and eventually the church itself. The cliff top is immediately behind the photographer.

The church never surrendered to the sea despite the loss of a corner of the churchyard in the 1950s. Since then, over the years the beach has steadily built up until today, when nature is reclaiming its hold on ground once lost – as seen here. Destroyed by a fire-bomb in 1942 and rebuilt after the war, All Saints' and St Margaret's remains – a symbol of the spirit of the people of Pakefield.

The ruins near All Saints' and St Margaret's Church, seen here from the Causeway in early 1978, were the remains of what had been a small group of ancient flintstone cottages adjacent to the north side of the churchyard. The outer shell of the cottage on the right survived until 1976, but by 1978 it had all but disappeared. Up until the nineteenth century Pakefield, like Lowestoft, had made much use of building material gathered from its beaches: by this date, however, most of the old village had all but gone with only a handful of the traditional cottages left.

Old cottages next to All Saints' and St Margaret's Church, *c.* 1930s. Taken in the depths of winter, looking across allotments and fields in the vicinity of what is now Sunningdale Avenue and facing east towards the North Sea, this amateur snapshot gives some idea of what the cottages in the previous scene would have looked like when they were inhabited.

Looking from the Causeway at the site of those cottages today. Both they and the tree were replaced by the house on the right in the 1980s. Utilising flintwork as part of its construction, it complements the church next door, itself rebuilt in 1949 after its destruction during the last war.

South Cliff Congregational church, *c.* 1905. On the corner of Pakefield Road and Morton Road not far from the Grand Hotel, it was designed by George Baines and Reginald Palmer of London. The church was dedicated in 1903 and included among its members chemist J.W. Dent, who was also the organist at the opening ceremony.

Little has changed over the years, apart from the boundary wall and the trees – but a declining congregation forced the church to close in 1995. It was bought by the Roman Catholic parish of Our Lady Star of the Sea to replace the small chapel in Blackheath Road, and after being ceremoniously handed over in August 1996 it was renamed St Nicholas' Church, South Cliff.

CHAPTER SEVEN

OULTON BROAD

John Garrity about to step on to *Grey Eagle* at Leo Robinson's
Broadside Yacht Station, 1930s. Based on the only Norfolk
Broad in Suffolk, Robinson's was one firm capitalising on the
arrival of the motor cruiser, then beginning to make its mark
on the Broad.

The junction of Normanston Drive and Gorleston Road, *c.* 1948. The main route to Lowestoft (right) is separated by a triangular green from Gorleston Road (known before the war as Yarmouth Road), leading to Oulton Village. The houses seen here were built in the 1930s. At this date both roads met in front of Holly Road, a few yards in front of Oulton Broad North station. (*Ann Hubbard*)

Today's scene is dominated by road signs and the roundabout, although a flower garden can still be found in the midst of the traffic flow, which has increased considerably over the years as the Broads have become more and more popular. Yesterday's cyclist felt a lot safer than the chap waiting to join the traffic on the right.

A bus waits at the junction of Fir Lane opposite the entrance to Normanston Park in Normanston Drive, March 1990. As late as the last decade much of Normanston Drive, the main route from Lowestoft to Oulton Broad, had managed to keep its rural character despite being part of Lowestoft since 1919. Only the bus shelter (centre right) gives any indication of the houses on both sides.

Today Peto Way cuts through Normanston Park and across Normanston Drive. Both roads meet at the roundabout (centre left), which also replaced the Fir Lane junction. Originally planned as a dual carriageway, the new road eventually comes out near Tesco's supermarket at Gunton.

Mutford Lock and the Wherry Inn, Mutford Bridge, from the Carlton Colville side, late 1860s. The Wherry was a favourite with yachtsmen and anglers as well as a halt for wherries travelling to Norwich. George Burrow lived nearby and possibly visited the inn. The lock in the foreground was built in 1828 as part of the navigable route from the new harbour at Lowestoft. (*Ray Vincent – Studio 161*)

The old bridge was built over the lock itself; later bridges were built on the Lake Lothing side. Looking across to Bridge Road today, this striking Dutch-style wooden footbridge built in the 1990s is not far from the location of that early bridge. Today's Wherry Hotel, built in 1897, is on the left.

Leo Robinson's Broadside Yacht Station, Oulton Broad, *c.* 1938. This was not long before the Second World War, when motor cruisers had almost superseded the old sailing wherries. At the height of the pre-war holiday trade, Robinson had also extended his house (centre), behind which is Caldecott Road.

Caldecott Road, the site of Robinson's boatyard – now Topcraft Cruisers – has changed almost out of all recognition. The Broads remain as popular with holidaymakers as they ever were, and like the yard the cruisers themselves have changed; glass-fibre replacing wood and colour television replacing the old wind-up gramophone.

Looking towards the Yacht Station and Nicholas Everitt Park, *c.* 1930. The Everitt estate next to the Broad had been bought by Howard Hollingsworth and given to the town as a park in 1929. The scene is unusually tranquil, so it is possibly the beginning of the season. The plaque in the foreground states that the pier (right) was given in memory of William Everitt.

Also photographed early in the season, small glass-fibre motor boats have superseded those wooden rowing-boats seen in days of yore. The most noticeable thing today is the height of the trees, obviously escaping the Hurricane of 1987. The plaque in the foreground is still there, although the quay (right) is now partly made of concrete.

A young lady stands on the deck of a cruiser moored at the Yacht Station, 1938. Looking beyond her and towards Mutford Lock reveals the construction of the road bridge opened in 1939, and there is a good view of the Lowestoft–Ipswich railway bridge (centre right). It is also worth speculating if the man in the yacht (left) had other things on his mind: he seems to be heading towards the pier!

Today's scene was taken early in the year – warm coats were needed that day. Looking from a similar position to the previous picture but on dry land, the view is nowadays dominated by the road bridge and bypass built in the early 1990s. Also seen here is the Dutch-style footbridge built at the same time. One of the popular Broads waterbuses is moored on the left.

Oulton Broad Swing Bridge, late 1980s. Built in 1939 to replace the previous bridge opened in 1894, it was one of only two bridges linking Lowestoft to the rest of Suffolk. Eventually it suffered from the strain of heavy traffic, and by the 1980s it became obvious that a new bridge was needed.

Today's bridge, part of a larger structure including lock, footbridge and bypass, was built across a stretch of Lake Lothing to the east of the previous bridge. The modern bypass remains one of only two road crossings connecting Lowestoft to the rest of Suffolk. The roof of the Wherry Hotel (left) can just about be seen through the collection of road signs.

L. and R. Taylor, newsagents and stationers on the corner of Bridge Road and Victoria Road, 1980s. Once Elliott's newsagents from the 1930s to the 1950s, Taylor's had moved there from London Road North when their previous shop was acquired for Tesco's supermarket expansion in the late 1970s. The shop in its turn was demolished in about 1990 to make way for the present bypass.

The site was not needed, and in 1999 a small housing complex was built in the shop's place, seen here framed between the traffic lights. Bridge Road is on the left – no longer clogged by traffic. Oulton Broad and its amenities are now approached by a slip-road from the bypass.

Douglas H. Blewitt, Victoria Road, *c.* 1934. From 1934 until 1938 Blewitt was an architect and estate agent at 157 Victoria Road. His was one of the many small firms building houses during the expansion of Oulton Broad in the years immediately before the war. He built homes on the Rock Estate as well as in Victoria Road and Kirkley Run, and may have built the workshop and office seen here.

Today 157 Victoria Road turned out to be quite a a surprise – at least to me – but the original shopfront is still there, albeit since the late 1930s with living accommodation over the top. Fred Smith had a fruiterer's shop here in 1938, later run by W.J. Oldham; and Mrs F. Blewitt had a grocery next door. Douglas Blewitt continued as a builder in Milton Road after the war.

Manual crossing, Victoria Road, *c.* 1980. Seen in the days before automatic barriers, this was Lowestoft's link with Ipswich and London. By this date, however, there were no longer direct connections with the capital and the line was about to become a single track with a semi-automated crossing. The shop next door, seen here as an upholsterer's, had at one time been a fishmonger's. (*Ray Vincent – Studio 161*)

The shop and the surrounding premises were demolished in about 1990 as part of the new road system. Today's busy crossing at Victoria Road features fully automatic barriers. Road traffic has mainly superseded rail and in the background a large roundabout now separates Victoria Road from Bridge Road.

Girls from the HDF no. 3 factory, Pye Television, School Road, 1950s. Pye came to the town in 1951 and took over the old Hinde silk works in School Road, which had been empty since the end of the war. Manufacturing radios and later televisions, Pye eventually became part of the Dutch Philips group in 1967. The factory closed in 1981. (*Russell Castleton*)

It was not long before the Japanese Sanyo company took over part of the old Pye factory, and also utilised the specialised skills of its workforce. Today School Road remains a centre for manufacturing quality televisions and video equipment.

ACKNOWLEDGEMENTS

I am indebted to those many people who passed on information or shared personal memories, and I would particularly like to thank the following for allowing me to use photographs in this book: Russell Castleton, Ann Hubbard, Mrs Ena Hall, Ian J. Mitchell, Waveney District Council, Richard Morling, and Mrs Joan Plant. I would like also to thank the Gunton Estate Tenants & Residents Association for information on the founding of the Gunton Estate and whose booklet *From Tin to Brick* celebrated its first fifty years; also to the staff of the Suffolk Records Office at Lowestoft for their help in answering any queries I had.

I would specially like to thank Ray Vincent of Studio 161 for his kind help and in allowing me to use photographs from his extensive collection. Thanks also to fellow members of the Jack Rose Old Lowestoft Society and notably to Jack Rose himself, who sadly died while I was compiling *Lowestoft Past and Present*. I would therefore like to acknowledge my own personal debt to Jack for his encouragement and help as well as words of guidance over the years, not only to myself but to all who shared his love of Lowestoft. His enthusiasm was infectious.

All other material comes from my archive, and as always I owe a final debt of gratitude to those photographers of the past, amateur or professional, known and unknown, without whom neither this book nor my archive would be possible.